E   C1

Downing, Joan.
        Baseball is our game

DATE DUE			

Baseball Is Our Game

By Joan Downing

Photographs by Tony Freeman

 CHILDRENS PRESS, CHICAGO

For Tracy, with love

Library of Congress Cataloging in Publication Data

Downing, Joan.
  Baseball is our game.

  Summary: A pictorial introduction to the game of
baseball.
  1. Baseball—Juvenile literature. [1. Base-
ball] I. Freeman, Tony, ill. II. Title.
GV867.5.D68   796.357'2   82-4418
ISBN 0-516-03402-2   AACR2

We play baseball.

Our coach talks to us
before each game.

When one team is on the field,
the other team is at bat.

The pitcher tries
to throw strikes.
If she throws
three strikes,
the batter is out.

The catcher wears
a mask,
shin guards,
and a chest protector.
The umpire wears them, too.

If the batter hits the ball,
he runs to first base.

12

We have to learn to catch the ball.

13

We have to learn
to throw the ball.

Pitching is
hard work.

Sometimes the runner is safe.

Sometimes he is out.

After three outs,
the other team is up.

We wait on the bench
for our turn at bat.

Our coaches help us during a game.

It is fun to get a hit.

Our safety helmets protect us.

We have to run fast.

Sometimes we hit well,
and run fast,
and touch all the bases.

Safe at home plate!
A run for our team!

Our families cheer.
Our friends cheer.

It doesn't matter
if we win or lose.
We love baseball!

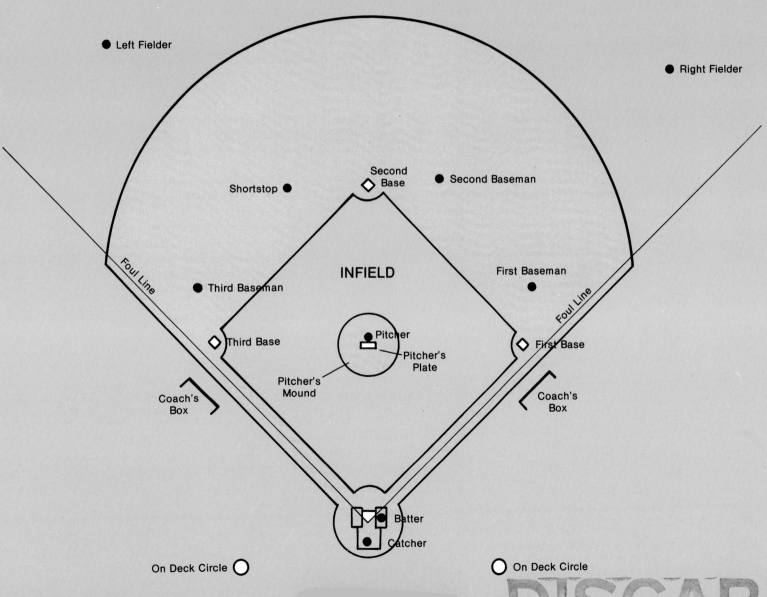

Center Fielder

OUTFIELD

Left Fielder

Right Fielder

Second Base

Shortstop ● Second Baseman

INFIELD

First Baseman

Third Baseman

Foul Line

Foul Line

Third Base

Pitcher

First Base

Pitcher's Plate

Pitcher's Mound

Coach's Box

Coach's Box

Batter

Catcher

On Deck Circle ○

○ On Deck Circle

About the Author

An experienced book editor and occasional freelance writer, **Joan Downing** has always been interested in and involved with books that deal with subjects that appeal to a broad spectrum of young readers. Her latest effort, *Baseball Is Our Game*, was written especially for those young people who are just beginning to acquire a real love of her favorite sport. Joan has worked in the graphic arts since her graduation from the University of Wisconsin in Madison. A resident of Evanston, Illinois, Joan currently shares her home with her daughter, Julie, and three cats of various sizes, shapes, colors, and personalities. Her sons, Tim and Chris, share a nearby apartment and are frequent visitors. Gardening, reading, summer fishing trips to Door County, Wisconsin, and winter craft projects top Joan's list of leisure-time activities.

About the Photographer

Tony Freeman has taught photography at Anaheim High School in Anaheim, California since 1962. He feels that he should remain active with photography if he is going to teach it. Add to this his interest in all of the exciting things the world has to offer, and it is obvious why he enjoys producing photographs and books. Mr. Freeman has always been active with his six children in Boy and Girl Scouting, school bands, sports, and church activities. He is around young people so much that he feels like one of them. So it was only natural that he turn to illustrating children's books. He gets great pleasure from learning new things and sharing these things with young people, both in his classroom and his books.